Bird Feeders and Shelters You Can Make

About the Book

Birds will come to your backyard and windowsill if you make them feel welcome. The most effective welcome is to provide the feeders and shelters birds can use. You can pick your favorite birds and encourage them to your backyard by the style and size of birdhouse you make and by the food you set out. The author tells you what food and what type of home to offer the various species of birds. There are also some hints on how to observe the birds as they go about setting up house and raising their young.

Eastern cowbird. (Other names: cow blackbird, lazybird, brown-headed blackbird, tickbird.) *Molothrus ater ater.*

English sparrow. (Other names: house sparrow, European house sparrow, domestic sparrow.) *Passer domesticus domesticus.*

Purple martin. (Other names: house martin, gourd martin, black martin.) *Progne subis subis.*

Wood thrush. (Other names: song thrush, wood robin, swamp angel, eeolee.) *Hylocichla mustelina.*

A CUB SCOUT PROJECT BOOK

Bird Feeders and Shelters

You Can Make

Ted S. Pettit

G. P. PUTNAM'S SONS, NEW YORK

Illustrations of Birds, courtesy, *Field Book of Eastern Birds,*
by Leon A. Hausman, G. P. Putnam's Sons

SBN: TR 399-20018-5

Fourth Impression

Copyright © 1970 by Boy Scouts of America

Library of Congress Catalog Card Number: 77-81660

PRINTED IN THE UNITED STATES OF AMERICA

07210

Two birds of mockingbird family.
Mimidae.

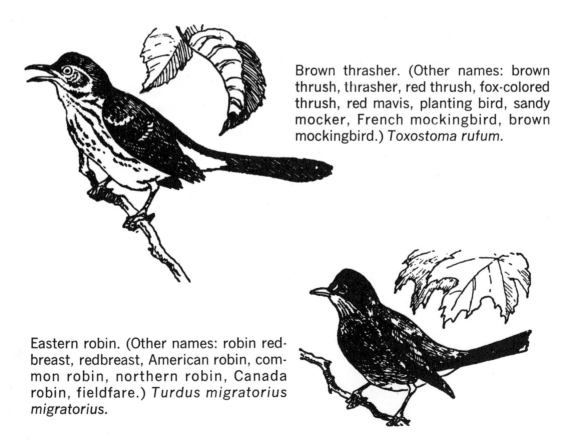

Brown thrasher. (Other names: brown
thrush, thrasher, red thrush, fox-colored
thrush, red mavis, planting bird, sandy
mocker, French mockingbird, brown
mockingbird.) *Toxostoma rufum.*

Eastern robin. (Other names: robin redbreast, redbreast, American robin, common robin, northern robin, Canada
robin, fieldfare.) *Turdus migratorius
migratorius.*

1 Bird Feeders and Shelters

Watching birds in your yard or a nearby park can be fun. It is more fun when you build your own feeder, nest box, or birdbath and watch birds using them. Almost anywhere you live—city, suburbs, or small town—there is something you can do to attract birds so that you can watch them more closely.

When birds come to a windowsill feeder or to a birdbath or nest in a box on a post nearby, they are easier to see and more fun to watch. Their colors seem brighter when they are closer to you, and the songs louder. Their markings, such as stripes, eye-rings, or wing bars, stand out so that it is easier to tell one bird from another.

Different birds have different ways of feeding, and you can see this easily when birds are close to you. Blue jays, for example, will hold a sunflower seed with their toes and pound it with their bills to open the shell. Cardinals and

Eastern goldfinch. (Other names: wild canary, yellowbird, thistlebird, catnip bird, shiner.) *Spinus tristis tristis.*

Catbird. (Other names: slate-colored mockingbird, gray mockingbird, black mockingbird, cat flycatcher, chicken bird.) *Dumatella carolinensis.*

Two birds of titmouse family. Paridae.

finches will pick up the seed in their bills, crack the shell, and remove the seed so fast you can hardly see what is going on.

Nuthatches many times cling to a feeder upside down to feed, and chickadees will hang on a feeder upside down, sideways, or up and down to get suet or peanut butter. Some birds will feed in small flocks, while others feed only one or two at a time. They try to drive away other birds that come while they are eating.

These are only some of the interesting things you can see when you watch birds close at hand. If you are lucky enough to have birds nest in a box you set out in the yard, there are other interesting things to see. You can watch the parent birds carry grass, straw, twigs, string, paper, feathers, or other materials into the box for the nest. Later you can watch them take insects to feed the young and, still later, watch them teach the young to fly. You may discover something about birds that no one else has found and be of help to science. You may even find that you want to make bird study your life's work or at least life-long hobby.

But before you start building feeders or nest boxes, it is important to know a little about birds in general and what they need to live.

You probably already know that some birds migrate. That is, birds such as robins, phoebes, and orioles fly south in the fall to spend the winter and fly north in the spring to nest. A few birds do not migrate but stay in one area the year round.

Generally, the birds you see may fall into one of four groups:

The first group consists of birds that live all year long in your area. Blue jays, cardinals, starlings, or titmice are examples of birds in this group.

The second group consists of birds that nest in your area but spend the winter south of where you live. Warblers, flycatchers, and orioles are in this class.

The third group is made up of birds that spend the summer north of you and the winter to the south. You see them briefly as they are flying through.

The last group is made up of birds that spend the winter in your area but nest far to the north. Evening grosbeaks or tree sparrows are examples of birds in this group.

What Birds Need

Birds, like other animals, need certain things in order to live. Knowing what these things are will help you know birds better and more easily attract them to your yard or other open area.

Food. Birds need food, lots of it. They are always hungry, it seems, and spend a large part of each day searching for the food they like. Some birds, such as sparrows, eat seeds mostly. In the wild they find weed or grass seeds in fields and along roadsides. Some of them will come to feeders containing seeds of several kinds. Other birds feed on insects and will come to feeders containing suet.

Water. Birds need water, for both drinking and bathing. Some get water from the food they eat, but others need water itself. A birdbath will attract some birds all year round.

Nesting Places. Birds need places to build their nests where they are safe from enemies or bad weather. Some birds nest in the branches of trees or shrubs and others on the ground or close to the ground. Some nest in hollow trees, and these birds many times use nest boxes placed outside for them.

Shelter. A place to hide from enemies or to find protection from bad weather is important to birds. They find shelter in dense shrubbery or in spruce or pine trees. In cities and towns, some birds, such as starlings, find shelter in the crevices of buildings or under the eaves of houses. You may be able to plant trees or shrubs or build a shelter for birds. Later on in this book you will find out how to do it.

Birds Are Always Hungry

The easiest way to attract birds is to build some feeders, set them out on posts or poles, and stock them with food. Late fall is a good time of year to start this project since natural food is harder to find then. But birds will come to feeders at any time of year, although it may take longer for them to discover a feeder in spring or summer than in fall or winter.

If you start feeding birds in late fall or winter, keep it up until late in the spring. When birds become accustomed to finding the food you put out and rely on finding it each day, they may have a hard time finding natural food if you stop feeding them.

Here are some of the different foods you can put out for birds and a list of some of the birds that may come to feed, depending on where you live.

Mixed seed. Many supermarkets, hardware stores, pet shops, department stores, and garden supply shops sell mixed birdseed. In the mixture may be cracked corn, sunflower seed, hemp, millet, or kafir corn. Birds that will eat it are cowbirds, redwings, fox sparrows, song sparrows, English sparrows, tree sparrows, catbirds, pine siskins, goldfinches, purple and house finches, titmice, and others.

Braces

Wood or Plastic Tray

Sunflower seed. Sunflower seed alone will attract many birds such as evening and pine grosbeaks, blue jays, Steller's jays, red-bellied woodpeckers, purple and house finches, chickadees, nuthatches, titmice, cardinals, goldfinches, and several kinds of sparrows.

Fruit. Cut-up pieces of fruit will be eaten by some birds that may not eat anything else. Cut-up apples, bananas, cranberries, raisins, or currants may attract mockingbirds, thrashers, catbirds, or bluebirds. But woodpeckers, myrtle

warblers, robins, hermit thrushes, and other birds will also eat fruit.

Suet. You can buy suet in any meat market, and ten cents' worth lasts a long time. Birds that eat it include white-breasted nuthatches, downy and hairy woodpeckers, Lewis' woodpeckers, red-breasted nuthatches, titmice, chickadees, flickers, brown creepers, kinglets, and starlings.

Peanut butter and nutmeats. These foods are easy to get, and you may already have them at home. Many birds will eat peanut butter or peanuts; they include nuthatches, woodpeckers, chickadees, titmice, catbirds, starlings, blackbirds, house or purple finches, and some of the sparrows.

Bread crumbs and odds and ends. Dry bread crumbs, stale doughnuts, stale fruitcake, cold cereals, and such odds and ends will also be eaten by many birds. Dry

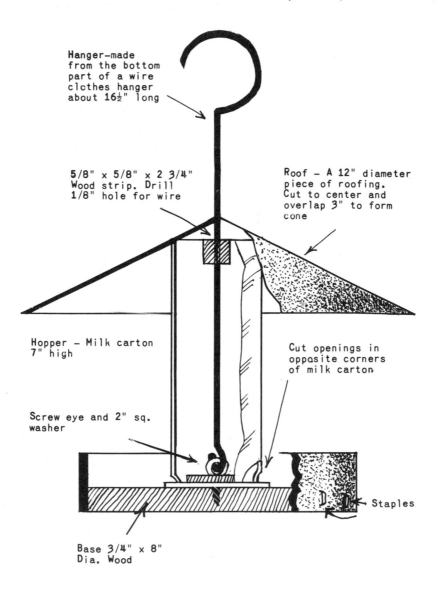

Hanger—made from the bottom part of a wire clothes hanger about 16½" long

5/8" x 5/8" x 2 3/4" Wood strip. Drill 1/8" hole for wire

Roof — A 12" diameter piece of roofing. Cut to center and overlap 3" to form cone

Hopper — Milk carton 7" high

Cut openings in opposite corners of milk carton

Screw eye and 2" sq. washer

Staples

Base 3/4" x 8" Dia. Wood

turkey or chicken dressing is also a good food. Almost any backyard bird will eat these odds and ends.

How to Make Bird Feeders

Bird feeders are easy to make, and it is best to start with a simple one. When you find that birds will come to your yard to feed, you can make a better feeder that will last a long time.

The easiest feeder to make is a simple tray about 18 inches long and 12 or 14 inches wide. You may have a flat wooden box you could use or even a plastic tray, such as those used in cafeterias.

Start by placing the tray on the ground near a tree or shrub, and put several kinds of food on the tray. In the beginning use bread crumbs, cold cereal, and other odds and ends. Watch the feeder once in a while for several days, and see if birds come to it.

You may find in some places that mice or dogs will come to eat the food before birds can find it. If that happens, place the tray on a post, as is shown in the pictures.

Even if you live in the city, you can still feed birds. Starlings and English sparrows live in cities, and so do pigeons. You may find a way of fastening a tray to a windowsill so that it cannot fall off, or if fire laws permit, you might place a tray on a fire escape. The building you live in may have a flat roof where a feeder might be placed.

Perhaps there is a park nearby where the officials would permit you to feed birds. Along the edges of cemeteries, golf courses, or other open areas near the city are also good places to put feeders.

If you do not have something to hold feed, make a simple tray. Get a board about 2 feet long and 10 inches wide. Some stores sell odd-size pieces of plywood. Then get some lath or similar wood 2 inches wide by 1/2 or 3/4 inch thick, and nail it around the edge of the board so the seed will not blow off. The picture shows how to do it.

A good trick also is to cut a mesh bag that some vegetables came in, so that it lies flat. Tack the mesh to the bottom of the tray on three sides so that it covers the food. Birds can peck through the mesh but can get only a little at a time, instead of flying off with too much. This is especially good if you use stale doughnuts, cake, or fruitcake.

The same kind of plastic mesh bag also makes a good feeder all by itself. Place a piece of suet, a stale doughnut, or stale fruitcake in the bag, and tie the top closed with a piece of string, using a bowknot like the one you use when you tie your shoes. Then it is easy to untie.

Hang the bag from tree or shrub, a clothesline post, or some other high place so that dogs cannot reach it. You could even hang it on the outside window frame if

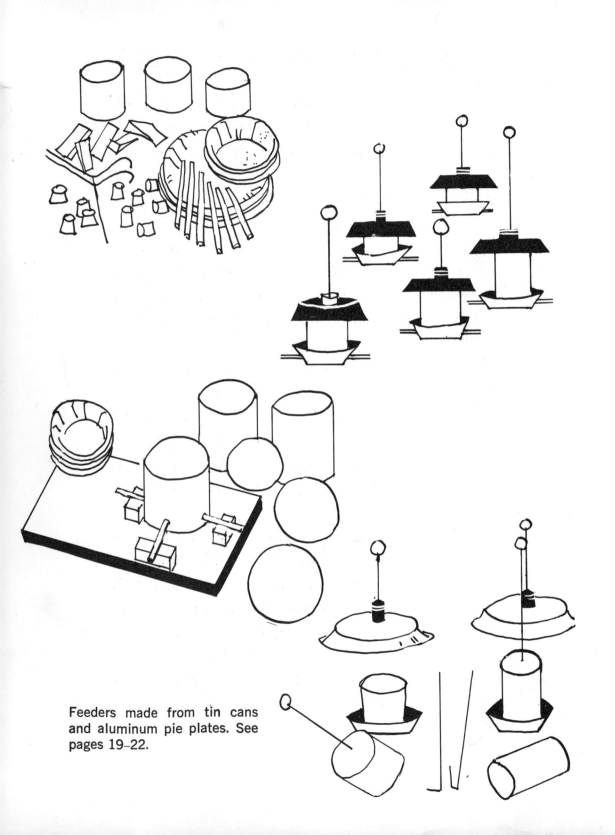

Feeders made from tin cans and aluminum pie plates. See pages 19–22.

your parents do not object. Birds can cling to the mesh while they peck at the food.

If you live in the city and have a clothesline outside the kitchen window, as some people have, you fasten the bag to the line with a clothespin and run it out from the window 10 feet or so.

Milk Carton Feeder

An easy-to-make feeder can be made from a half-gallon or one-gallon milk container. It will not last as long as a wooden one, but then a milk carton is easy to get, and you can replace it every week or so. This feeder is good for seed.

Cut a hole in the carton about two inches from the bottom through which birds can get food. Fasten or glue a square piece of wood to the bottom for birds to perch on. Cut a small hole in the top, and use string or wire to hang the feeder from a branch or nail on a post.

Tin Can Feeders

Other hanging feeders can be made from tin cans, the aluminum-foil plates that pies come in, some wire coat hangers, and a few one-inch corks.

Two-pound coffee cans or similar-size tin or other con-

Glass jar feeder. See page 22.

tainers are a good size. You will need 9-inch foil plates
and 6-inch plates.

First, use the kind of can opener that cuts a triangular
hole in a can, and make five openings in the side of the can
just above the bottom rim.

Next, straighten or cut a wire coat hanger so you have

20

a piece of wire 18 inches long. Bend a loop in one end of the wire.

Cut a hole the size of the wire in the exact center of a 6-inch aluminum-foil plate. Cut a similar hole in the center of a 9-inch plate. Cut another hole in the center of the bottom of the can.

With the 6-inch plate right side up, push the wire through the hole in the plate, through the hole in the can, and through the hole in the 9-inch plate with the plate upside down. Fill the can with mixed birdseed, and check to see that the seed falls out through the holes onto the bottom plate. Then force a cork down the wire until it is tight against the top plate. Form a hook in the top end of the wire, and hang the feeder on a tree branch or clothesline.

Another kind of automatic feeder can be made from a glass jar, a piece of inner tube, and a board. With this kind of feeder you can see how much seed is inside at all times.

The materials you need are: a 1-inch board, 12 inches by 18 inches; a large glass jar; some tacks; a strip of inner tube or similar rubber; and a post.

Place the jar, open end down, in the center of the board. Draw around the edge with a pencil. Mark a section about 1¼ inches wide, as shown. Use a hammer and large screwdriver or chisel to gouge out holes, as shown. Be sure the outside end is deeper so the seed can roll out.

Then cut some strips of wood, and form a rim around

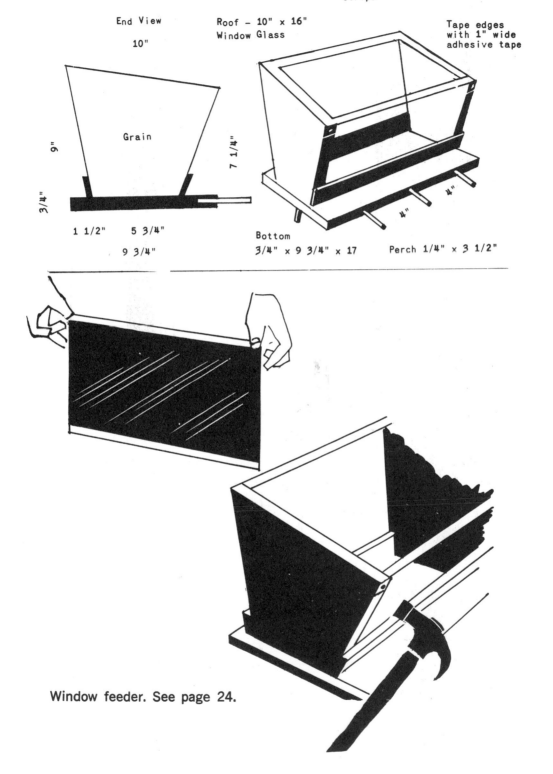

End View

10"

Roof — 10" x 16"
Window Glass

1/4" x 1 1/2" x 16"
strips

Tape edges
with 1" wide
adhesive tape

9"

Grain

7 1/4"

3/4"

1 1/2"   5 3/4"

9 3/4"

Bottom
3/4" x 9 3/4" x 17

4"

4"

Perch 1/4" x 3 1/2"

Window feeder. See page 24.

the cutout sections so the ends of the rim match the outer edge of the jar.

Cut a piece of 1½-foot-wide rubber twice as long as the jar. Fasten the two ends to the board with strips of wood and small nails. Make a railing around the board to keep the seed from blowing away. Fasten the board to the post.

Fill the jar with seed, place it on the board, secure it with the rubber, and you are ready to entertain birds.

Window Feeder

With a windowsill feeder you can really see birds close at hand, especially if the top is made of glass.

Materials needed are: a 1-inch board, 10 inches by 37 inches; two ¼-by-1½-inch wood strips; a 10-by-16-inch piece of window glass; some 1-inch-wide waterproof adhesive or electrical tape; one ¼-inch dowel or piece of round wood; a few nails; and four upholsterer's nails.

First paint or stain the wood. Then follow the directions with the pictures.

A Pulley Feeder

Sometimes birds are too wary to come to your windowsill and require a little coaxing. That is when a pulley feeder comes in handy. You can start it 20 feet or so away

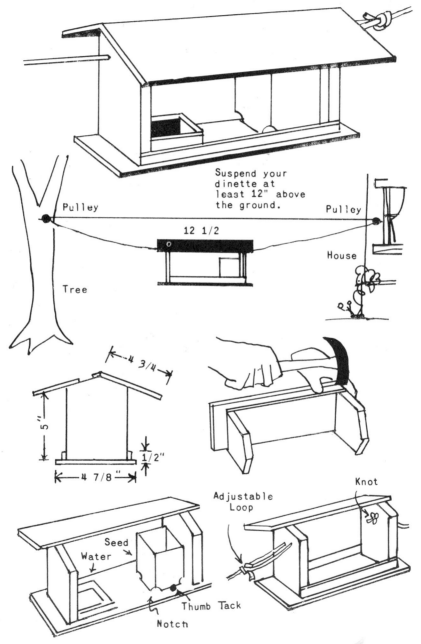

Suspend your
dinette at
least 12" above
the ground.

Pulley

Pulley

12 1/2

Tree

House

4 3/4

5 "

1/2"

4 7/8 "

Seed
Water

Thumb Tack

Notch

Adjustable
Loop

Knot

Pully feeder. See page 24.

from the window and wait until birds start to use it regularly. Then you can pull it in a few inches each day until the birds are just outside the window.

Scrap wood can be used, or you can buy the wood you need at a lumber yard. The pictures show how to make it.

Weather Vane Feeder

When you find that backyard bird watching is fun and that birds come regularly to your feeders, you may want

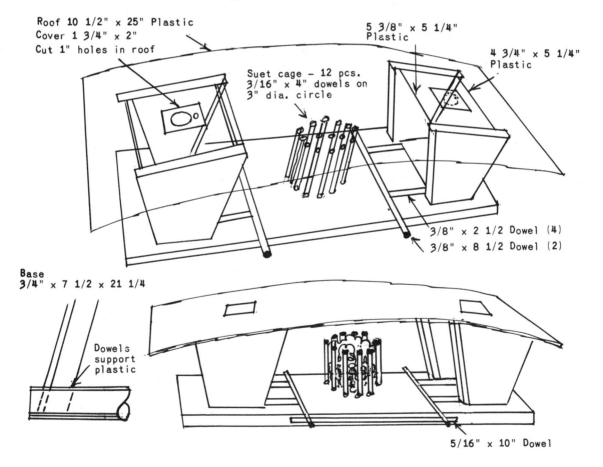

Roof 10 1/2" x 25" Plastic
Cover 1 3/4" x 2"
Cut 1" holes in roof

5 3/8" x 5 1/4" Plastic

4 3/4" x 5 1/4" Plastic

Suet cage — 12 pcs.
3/16" x 4" dowels on
3" dia. circle

3/8" x 2 1/2 Dowel (4)
3/8" x 8 1/2 Dowel (2)

Base
3/4" x 7 1/2 x 21 1/4

Dowels
support
plastic

5/16" x 10" Dowel

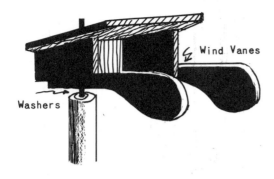

Washers

Wind Vanes

to make a permanent feeder built like a weather vane. This type of feeder turns in the wind so that the open side always faces away from the wind. Snow doesn't blow in and the seed doesn't blow out.

The window feeder described on page 24 can be made into a weather vane feeder by making the back of glass and the top of wood. Make two wings as shown, and nail them to the sides of the feeder.

Set a post in the ground. Get a piece of aluminum rod, ⅜ or ½ inch in diameter, at a hardware store. Drill a hole in the top of the post, and insert the rod. Tap the rod gently with a hammer. Place two or three washers over the rod.

Cut holes in the center of the bottom and top of the feeder, and slide the feeder down the rod.

Suet Feeders

Insect-eating birds, such as woodpeckers, generally prefer suet or other animal fat, so be sure to make a suet

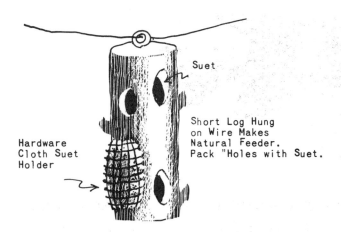

Suet

Short Log Hung
on Wire Makes
Natural Feeder.
Pack "Holes with Suet.

Hardware
Cloth Suet
Holder

feeder or two if you want these birds to come to the yard.

The simplest suet feeder is a mesh bag filled with suet and hung on a branch or nail on a post.

Another kind can be made by first fastening a wire or plastic soap dish to a board as shown and then nailing the board to a post or tree.

Another kind that is easy to make requires a piece of tree branch with bark on, about 18 inches long and 3 inches in diameter. Drill 1-inch holes in the log, and stuff pieces of suet in the holes. Fasten a screw eye in one end, and hang it up. If you use a piece of planed lumber, 2 inches by 2 inches by 18 inches, roughen the wood with a chisel or screwdriver under the holes so birds have something to cling to.

In cities and towns, starlings will come to suet feeders regularly. But in some places, starlings may be a nuisance and drive away other birds that you want to watch.

Here is a good way to discourage starlings if you do not want them.

Use 1-by-4-inch lumber or scrap boards to make an open-ended box about 4 inches square and 6 inches long. Fasten a piece of hardware cloth or plastic mesh bag on one end. Cut a piece of wood so it fits loosely inside the other end and will slide up and down. Use a 1-inch screw eye or a nail for a handle so you can remove the wood.

Put two screw eyes opposite each other, as shown, and hang the feeder with the mesh end down. Place suet in the box, and push down with the plunger to force it to the bottom. Starlings will not usually use this kind of feeder.

Suet feeders. See page 28.

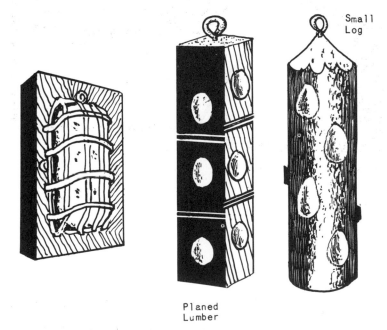

Small Log

Planed Lumber

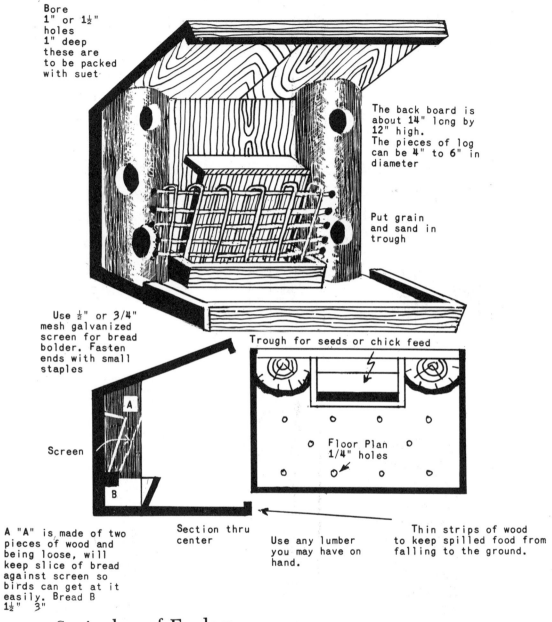

Bore 1" or 1½" holes 1" deep these are to be packed with suet

The back board is about 14" long by 12" high.
The pieces of log can be 4" to 6" in diameter

Put grain and sand in trough

Use ½" or 3/4" mesh galvanized screen for bread bolder. Fasten ends with small staples

Trough for seeds or chick feed

Screen

A

B

Floor Plan 1/4" holes

A "A" is made of two pieces of wood and being loose, will keep slice of bread against screen so birds can get at it easily. Bread B 1½" 3"

Section thru center

Use any lumber you may have on hand.

Thin strips of wood to keep spilled food from falling to the ground.

Squirrel-proof Feeders

In some cases, squirrels may be a real nuisance. They eat large amounts of food and, while they are in a feeder, keep birds away. If you have this problem, here is a way to keep squirrels out of hanging feeders.

Place two posts in the ground so the tops are about 8 feet above the ground and 10 feet apart. Get an 11-foot-long piece of thin, but strong wire, and fasten one end to the top of one post. Then get some inexpensive

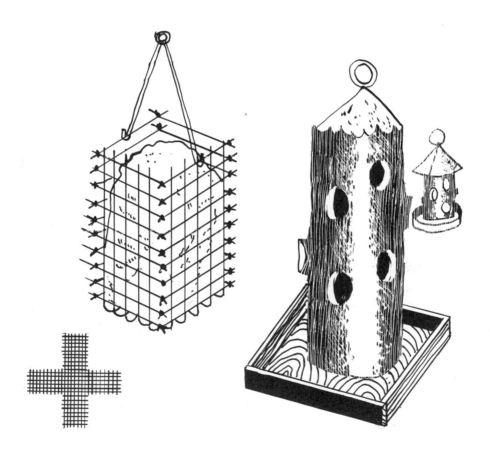

Squirrel-proof feeders.

Two birds of finch family. Fringillidae.

Eastern bluebird. (Other names: blue redbreast, common bluebird, blue robin, Wilson's bluebird.) *Sialia sialis sialis.*

Barn owl. (Other names: monkey-faced owl, golden owl, white owl.) *Tyto alba pratincola.*

Simple suet feeder. See page 28.

dime-store glass beads that will fit the wire. String enough on the wire to cover 18 inches of it close to the first post. Keep the beads in place with a piece of tape wrapped around the wire. Do the same thing at the other end, and fasten the wire to the second post. Hang your feeders from the wire in between the beads. As a squirrel tries to walk the wire from the post, the beads turn, and he falls off.

Ground-feeding Birds

Some birds prefer to feed on the ground, and although they will feed at feeders, they will be attracted more

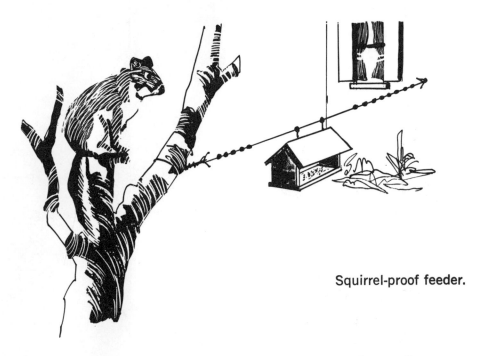

Squirrel-proof feeder.

quickly if you feed them on the ground, where they are accustomed to feed naturally. Some of the sparrows, juncos, cowbirds, and doves are in this class.

Old Christmas trees make fine ground feeders. Chop off the branches from one side, and save them. Drive a stake in the ground so that it sticks up about 2 feet above the ground. Nail the bottom of the tree to the top of the post so that the small end of the tree is on the ground and the side from which you cut branches is down.

Use the branches you cut off to cover any open places in the tree. Sprinkle food in front of and under the tree. The tree will provide protection from wind and snow. But if there are cats around, don't make this kind of feeder. It's too easy for the cats to catch the birds.

How to Feed Birds in the House

If your mother doesn't object, and she probably won't, here's a stunt that will enable you to attract birds within the house. Blue jays and even cowbirds or sparrows will do it quite readily.

Ground feeders. See pages 33–34.

Start with peanuts for jays or seeds for sparrows or cowbirds, and attract birds to your windowsill. After the birds come regularly and feed without fear, open the window a little. When they get used to that, open the window still further. Finally, get them accustomed to feeding on the windowsill with the window wide open. It may take several days, with an hour or two a day getting them used to the open window. Next, move the feed from the feeder to the inside windowsill, and give the birds time to become used to feeding on the sill just inside the window.

Christmas tree ground feeder. See page 34.

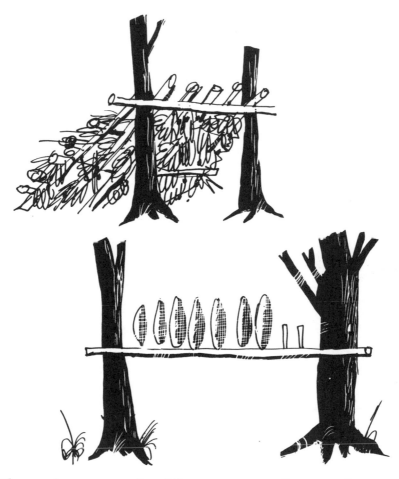

Then place a card table or some other easily moved table up against the inside windowsill, and put the food on the table near the window. When the birds become accustomed to feeding in the house on the table, move the food across the table to the other side. In a few days, you can move the table back into the room a few feet. Finally, birds will fly to the window, perch on the sill, look into the room, fly in after food, and fly out the window again.

White-breasted nuthatch. (Other names: common nuthatch, white-bellied nuthatch, whitebreast, Carolina nuthatch, tree mouse, devil down-head, upside-down bird, sapsucker, topsy-turvy bird.) *Sitta carolinensis carolinensis.*

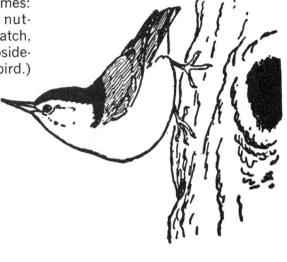

Red-breasted nuthatch. (Other names: red-bellied nuthatch, redbreast, Canada nuthatch.) *Sitta canadensis.*

Northern blue jay. (Other names: jay, jaybird, bluecoat, corn thief, nest robber.) *Cyanocitta cristata cristata.*

Eastern cardinal. (Other names: cardinal grosbeak, Kentucky cardinal, redbird, Virginia, redbird, crested redbird.) *Richmondena cardinalis cardinalis.*

If you sit very quietly, not moving a muscle, they will even fly in while you are there and feed right before your eyes, almost from your own dining-room table. It's an interesting trick and a lot of fun.

How to Feed Birds from Your Hand

Even more fun is feeding birds right from your hand. Here's how to do it.

Start by attracting birds to your windowsill, and wait until they are accustomed to feeding there. Then get a piece of wood about 1 inch by 2 inches and 2 or 3 feet long. Also, get an old pair of gloves or a pair of inexpensive cotton work gloves.

Put one glove on the end of the wood, and fasten it with a thumbtack. Slide the sleeve of an old coat or sweater on the wood so the sleeve comes right to the glove.

Push this "arm"—sleeve and glove—out the window, and put the window down so it holds the "arm" in place, sticking out over the window feeder. Sprinkle some food on the glove. Leave it there for a week or so until the birds are used to it and eat the seed from the glove.

Then substitute your own arm for the wood. Put on the coat or sweater and the glove, and poke your arm out the window.

Rest your arm on the windowsill so it won't get tired, and fill the palm of the glove with seed.

Feeding birds from your hand.

Very soon the birds will start eating right from your hand. The next step is to remove the glove and let the birds feed from your bare hand. That's really fun.

One bird watcher did it a little differently. He built a scarecrow out in his yard, using old clothes and an old hat to cover a wooden frame. The arms were outstretched. He put feed on the hat and in the hands, on the shoulders, and even in a corncob pipe in the scarecrow's mouth. After a few weeks, birds were feeding all over the scarecrow—sitting on the hat, the shoulders, and the arms and even feeding out of the corncob pipe.

One night the bird watcher took the scarecrow indoors and took off the clothes. The next morning at dawn he took the place of the scarecrow, wearing exactly the same clothes. Sure enough, the birds came quite readily and perched all over him as they fed on the food he had provided.

Flycatcher family. Tyrannidae.

Two birds of wood warbler family. Compsothlypidae.

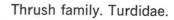

Thrush family. Turdidae.

Eastern winter wren. (Other names: short-tailed wren, spruce wren, wood wren, mouse wren.) *Nannus hiemalis hiemalis.*

II Bird Boxes

Why Birdhouses Are Necessary

Strange as it may seem, many birds have no place to nest just because people are too neat. It works like this: Birds such as bluebirds, chickadees, woodpeckers, flickers, tree swallows, crested flycatchers, screech owls, and other birds nest in holes in trees. But when trees die in our yards, parks, or wooded areas, we cut them down. We just do not like to see dead trees. Our neatness means that some birds have fewer homes, and since these birds will nest nowhere else except in holes in trees or in bird boxes, frequently the birds become quite rare in some localities as nesting species.

It's easy to build and set out bird boxes, and it's fun. More than that, it may well be responsible for increasing the number of certain birds which have been rare in your area.

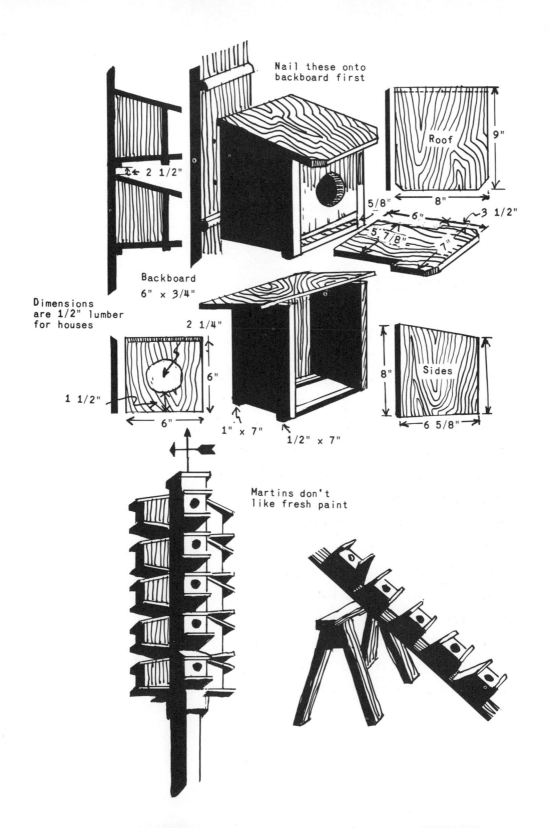

Nail these onto
backboard first

Roof

9"

5/8"

6"

3 1/2"

8"

5 7/8"

7"

2 1/2"

Backboard
6" x 3/4"

Dimensions
are 1/2" lumber
for houses

2 1/4"

6"

6"

1 1/2"

6"

Sides

8"

6 5/8"

1" x 7"

1/2" x 7"

Martins don't
like fresh paint

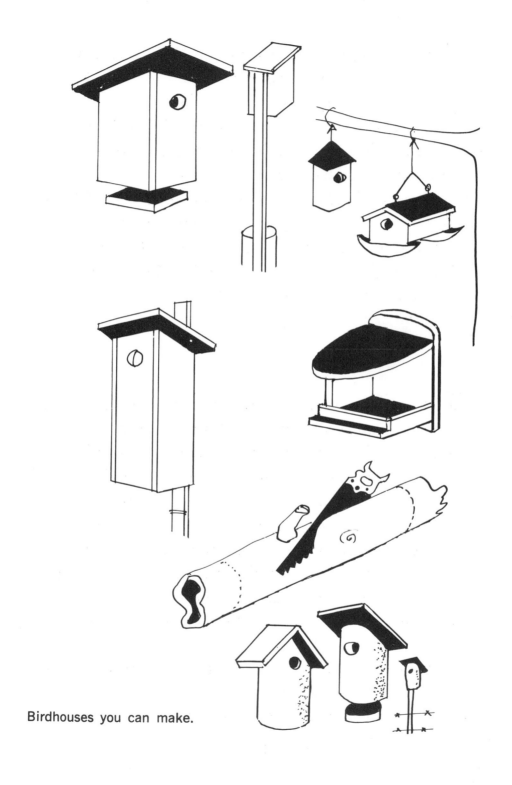

Birdhouses you can make.

A few years ago a Boy Scout troop in northern Michigan was directly responsible for a huge increase in the number of bluebirds in the area. They did it first by building and setting out more than 150 bluebird houses—and then by cleaning out and repairing the houses each fall after the birds had left.

On Cape Cod, Massachusetts, another group of boys was successful in getting tree swallows to nest where previously they had not been known except as migrants passing through. Again the secret was building and setting out suitable nesting boxes.

Where to Put Birdhouses

Bird boxes may be put up almost anywhere, and it is amazing how quickly they will attract occupants. A few years ago a fellow working on a Boy Scout merit badge looked for a place to set out some nesting boxes. He lived in the middle of a large city, where there wasn't even a suitable park. One day he passed a cemetery and saw that there were lots of trees there and that it was apparently a good place for birds if they had places to nest. The cemetery officials readily gave permission for the birdhouses, and he set them out. Out of eighteen houses, ten were used the first year, by house wrens, chickadees, and downy woodpeckers One starling family took over one house, and English sparrows occupied two.

In other places, the rows of trees between the fairways

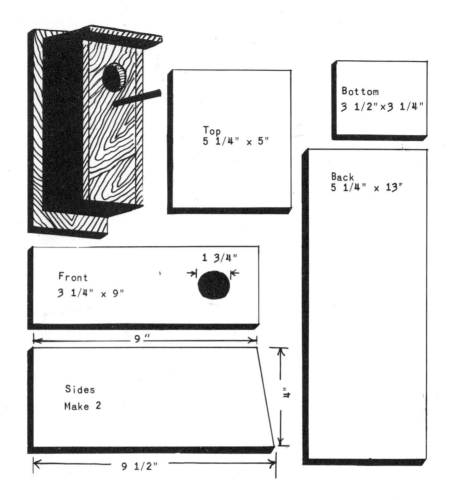

Top
5 1/4" x 5"

Bottom
3 1/2" x 3 1/4"

Back
5 1/4" x 13"

Front
3 1/4" x 9"

1 3/4"

9"

Sides
Make 2

4"

9 1/2"

A bird box.

on golf courses have been used successfully for birdhouses, and in the more open country, fence posts along roadsides, trees in apple orchards, and posts or trees along the edge of woodlots or hedgerows. There are many places where birdhouses may be set out, but most important are the specifications of the houses themselves.

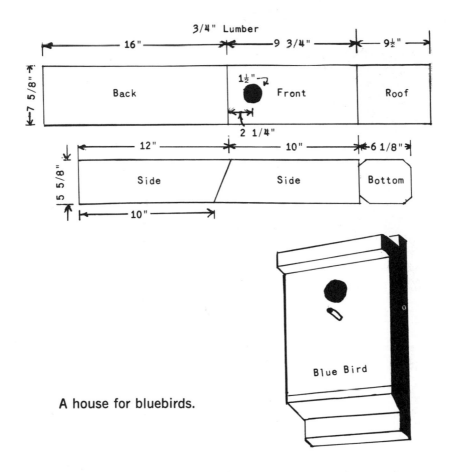

A house for bluebirds.

General Requirements of Successful Birdhouses

Cities, villages, towns, and counties frequently have building codes that set forth how houses for human occupants must be built. Certain specifications must be met before the houses may be occupied. These codes are designed to protect the safety of the people who live in the houses. Birds themselves have certain requirements for their homes, or they will not move in. Then, too, other requirements must be met for the protection of the birds.

Building bird boxes may be a complete waste of time, money, and energy if, after the houses are built, birds will not use them or if they do use them but do not successfully raise a crop of young.

Here are some general rules to follow:

1. Make the houses for specific birds—wood duck boxes, chickadee boxes, bluebird houses. Do not make just "birdhouses."

2. Do not try bird apartment houses, except for martins. Most birds demand privacy and will drive away others that come too close to their houses.

3. Make the holes to fit the bird. Every bird has its own requirements. With songbird houses, English sparrows or starlings will move in and drive away more desirable birds if the hole is large enough. With wood duck boxes, raccoons may get in and destroy the eggs or young ducks if the hole is not just right.

4. Do not use tin cans as a general rule. The sun beating down may heat the inside like an oven and bake the young birds.

5. Do not set up too many houses in a small area. Three or four to an acre is the largest number that will be used.

6. Do not hide the houses in dense foliage. They should be placed in open shade, on poles, or tree trunks or suspended from branches.

7. Clean out the houses after each season. Birds demand clean houses each year. This means that boxes

Species	Floor of Cavity	Depth of Cavity	Entrance Above Floor	Dia of Entrance
Blue Bird	5" x 5"	8"	6"	1 1/2"
Chickadee	4" x 4"	8" – 10"	6" – 8"	1 1/8"
Titmouse	4" x 4"	8" – 10"	6" – 8"	1 1/4"
Nuthatches	4" x 4"	8" – 10"	6" – 8"	1 1/4"
House Wren	4" x 4"	6" – 8"	1" – 6"	7/8"
Carolina Wren	4" x 4"	6" – 8"	1" – 6"	1 1/8"
Crested Flycatcher	6" x 6"	8" – 10"	6" – 8"	2"
Flicker	7" x 7"	16" – 18"	14" – 16"	2 1/2"
Red–Headed Woodpecker	6" x 6"	12" – 15"	9" – 12"	2"
Downy Woodpecker	4" x 4"	8" – 10"	6" – 8"	1 1/4"
Purple Martin	6" x 6"	6"	1"	2 1/2"
Tree Swallow	5" x 5"	6"	1" – 5"	1 1/2"
Barn Owl	10" x 18"	15" – 18"	4"	6"
Sparrow Hawk	8" x 8"	12" – 15"	9" – 12"	3"

should have provisions for easy cleaning. The tops or bottoms should be either hinged or fastened with an easily removable screw so that they may be cleaned without being taken down.

8. All houses should be made so that they are well ventilated and easily drained of any rainwater that may blow in. Slits under the roof provide ventilation, and a few holes drilled in the bottom will provide drainage.

Birdhouse Sizes for Common Species

Following are specifications for houses for some of the more common species, recommended by the U.S. Department of Agriculture:

1. Bluebird, mountain bluebird, western bluebird, house finch

Floor size	5 by 5 inches
Height of house	8 inches
Hole above floor	6 inches
Diameter of hole	1½ inches
Height above ground	5 to 10 feet

For bluebirds, place the houses in sunny places, in orchards, or along roadsides. For house finches, place them in yards or gardens.

2. House wren, Carolina wren

Floor size	4 by 4 inches
Height of house	6 or 8 inches

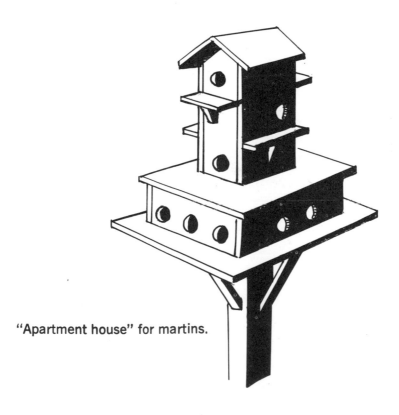

"Apartment house" for martins.

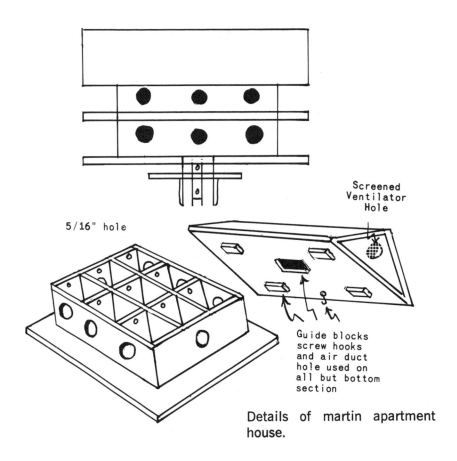

5/16" hole

Screened
Ventilator
Hole

Guide blocks
screw hooks
and air duct
hole used on
all but bottom
section

Details of martin apartment house.

Hole above floor	6 inches
Diameter of hole	1 inch
Height above ground	5 to 10 feet

For Carolina wrens, make the hole 1⅛ inches. Set out the houses in the very early spring and not too close together.

3. Chickadee, nuthatch, titmouse, downy woodpecker

Floor size	4 by 4 inches
Height of house	8 to 10 inches
Diameter of hole	1⅛ inches

Hole above floor   6 to 8 inches

Height above ground   5 to 15 feet

For nuthatches, titmice, and woodpeckers, make the hole 1¼ inches. All these birds prefer bark-covered houses. Use slab wood with bark on it, or drill a hole through a log. For downies, place some wood chips in the bottom.

4. Tree swallow, violet-green swallow

Floor size	5 by 5 inches
Height of house	6 inches
Diameter of hole	1½ inches
Hole above floor	5 inches
Height above ground	5 to 15 feet

Place these houses in the open on a post or dead tree.

5. Crested flycatcher

Floor size	6 by 6 inches
Height of house	8 to 10 inches
Diameter of hole	2 inches
Hole above floor	6 to 8 inches
Height above ground	8 to 20 feet

Make the house of wood at least an inch thick. Sprinkle chips or shavings inside.

6. Screech owl

Floor size	8 by 10 inches
Height of house	12 to 15 inches
Diameter of hole	3¼ inches
Hole above floor	10 inches

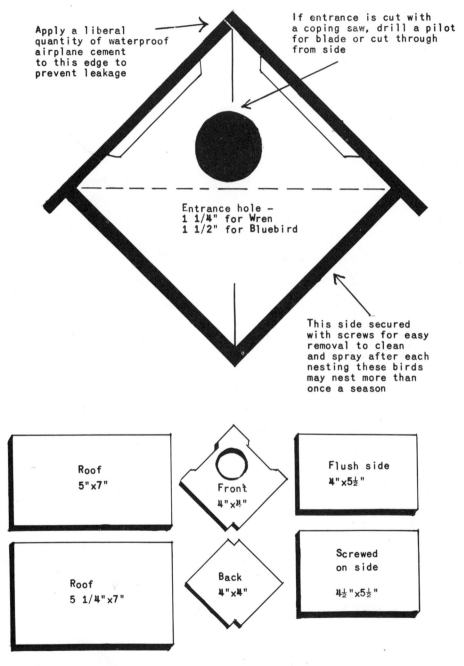

Apply a liberal
quantity of waterproof
airplane cement
to this edge to
prevent leakage

If entrance is cut with
a coping saw, drill a pilot
for blade or cut through
from side

Entrance hole –
1 1/4" for Wren
1 1/2" for Bluebird

This side secured
with screws for easy
removal to clean
and spray after each
nesting these birds
may nest more than
once a season

Roof
5"x7"

Front
4"x4"

Flush side
4"x5½"

Roof
5 1/4"x7"

Back
4"x4"

Screwed
on side
4½"x5½"

House for wrens or bluebirds.

Height above ground   10 to 30 feet

A rustic house is best, but even then, it takes luck to get one to use it.

How to Make a Basic Bird Box

One of the best all-around bird boxes can be made rather quickly. Here's how to do it:

Use 1-inch-thick wood, which is ¾ to ⅞ of an inch thick, as you get it from the lumberyard. Use brass screws and hinges so they will not rust.

To make one house, you will need a piece of wood 6 inches wide (about 5¾ inches as is comes from the mill) and 52 inches long. Saw off a piece 14 inches long for the backboard. Saw off a second piece 5 inches long for the top, and cut it down to 5 inches by 5¼ inches.

Then ripsaw the board for 19 inches so you have a piece 4 inches wide. Cut this piece into two 9½-inch pieces for the sides. Saw a ½-inch triangle off each side so the top will slant toward the front.

Next, rip the board so you have a piece 3¼ inches wide. Cut off a piece 9 inches long for the front and a piece 3¼ inches square for the bottom. The bottom and the front fit inside the sides. Center the sides on the backboard, and use screws to fasten in place. Use a hinge to attach the top to the backboard. Be careful drilling the hole so as not to split the front. With a 1½-inch hole,

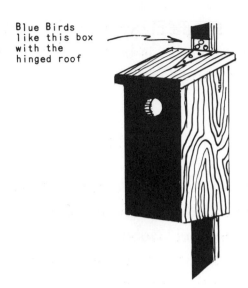

Blue Birds
like this box
with the
hinged roof

this box is suitable for bluebirds or tree swallows. With a 1-inch hole, it will do for a house wren. Different sizes make it suitable for different birds.

Wood Duck Boxes

The general principles for building wood duck boxes are the same as for any bird box. But the size specifications are much larger:

Floor area	10 by 10 inches
Height of house	28 inches
Hole diameter	3 by 5 inches (oval-shaped)
Hole above floor	20 inches
Height above ground	6 to 20 feet

The house may be placed on pole which has been

driven into mud in the bottom of a lake or pond or in trees near the water's edge. Very important: Place 4 inches of sawdust in the house, and tack screening or hardware cloth inside the front so the young ducks can climb up to the hole.

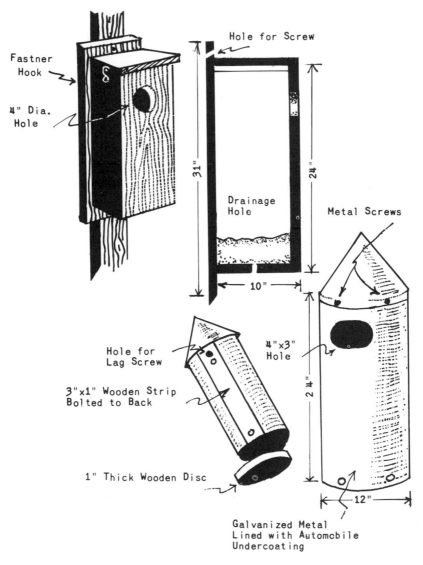

Two boxes for wood ducks.

If the houses are placed on poles, tack sheet metal or tin around the pole for 12 to 20 inches under the house so raccoons cannot climb up and get at the eggs or young birds.

Select a marshy or brushy area so ducks can feed and rest on the water in a protected place. Place the boxes above possible floodwater height.

How to Build a Nesting-Material Box

Some birds will not nest in birdhouses, but you can still help them. Make a rack, as shown, and fill it with bits of string, yarn, pieces of grass, moss, or other materials that birds such as robins, orioles, thrashers, and catbirds will use in nest building.

To make such a rack, use wood ¼ inch by 2 inches wide. Cut two strips 10 inches long and two pieces 6 inches long. Nail them together so that you have a 2-inch-deep box without a top or bottom. Tack fine-mesh hardware cloth on the box to form a top and bottom. Or you may use a long piece of wire and wrap it around the box several times to form a grille over the open sides.

Then fill the box with nesting materials, and hang it in a tree or from a post where birds can get at it and pick out the pieces of string or yarn. When you fill the box, be sure that the string or yarn is in short pieces, 6 to 8 inches long.

Part of the fun comes from watching birds pull out the string and carry it to their nests. But the real fun comes in the fall, when you take down the old nest and examine it carefully. If the string or yarn is of different colors or kinds, you'll be able to follow one piece through the complicated weaving job that the bird does and see exactly how it made the nest.

How to Help Robins and Phoebes Build Homes

Robins will not nest in birdhouses, but they will sometimes nest on a bracket or shelf set up in a tree. The illustration shows how to make a robin bracket.

Use wood from the ends of an old apple crate or any other wood that is about 1 inch thick and 6 inches wide. Cut one piece 6 inches long for a base; a piece 8 inches long for the back; and a piece 8 inches long for the roof. Nail the back to the floor, and then nail on the roof so it slants downward slightly toward the front. Use pieces of

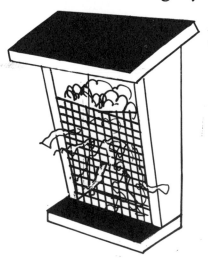

Rack with nesting materials for robins and other birds. See pages 58–59.

wood ½ inch by 2 inches to make a lip around the floor and to support the roof.

Place this bracket 10 to 15 feet up in a tree, and fasten it securely.

Phoebes are birds that frequently nest under bridges. They will build their nests up against the rafters or stringers of wooden bridges or even on the ledges of I beams on steel bridges.

In many places they will nest up under the eaves of a house or garage if a suitable spot is available. Generally, all that is necessary is a 4- to 6-inch-wide board fastened to the house or garage up close to the eaves. Since phoebes nest early and raise two or three broods of young each year, you may have a lot of fun watching them if you are successful in attracting them.

Easy-to-Make Bird Boxes

One of the easiest birdhouses to make, if you have an old flowerpot or can get one, is this: Use a clay flowerpot

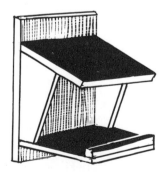

A bracket with roof for nesting robins.

that is about 8 inches in diameter and about 8 inches deep, with a 1-inch hole in the bottom. Get a square piece of board about an inch larger than the open end of the pot.

Lay the board on the floor, and place the open end of the flowerpot on the board. Get some nails just long enough to go from the ridge around the pot halfway through the board.

Carefully hammer about six nails into the board around

Blackbird family. Icteridae.

Eastern sparrow hawk. (Other names: killy hawk, kitty hawk, American kestrel, grasshopper hawk, mouse hawk, windhover, rusty-crowned falcon.) *Falco sparverius sparverius.*

Eastern phoebe. (Other names: bridge bird, pewee, bridge pewee, water pewee, barn pewee, pewit, water pewit, pewit flycatcher, bean bird, dusky flycatcher.) *Sayornis phoebe.*

Eastern warbling vireo. (Other name: warbling greenlet.) *Vireo gilvus gilvus.*

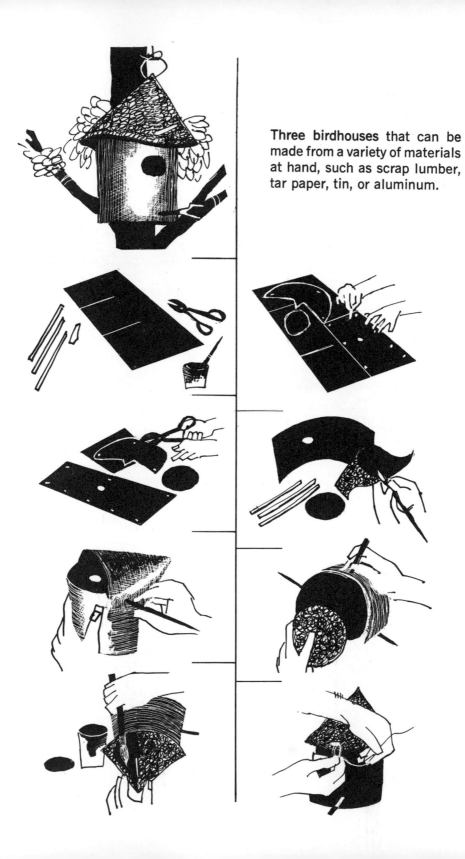

Three birdhouses that can be made from a variety of materials at hand, such as scrap lumber, tar paper, tin, or aluminum.

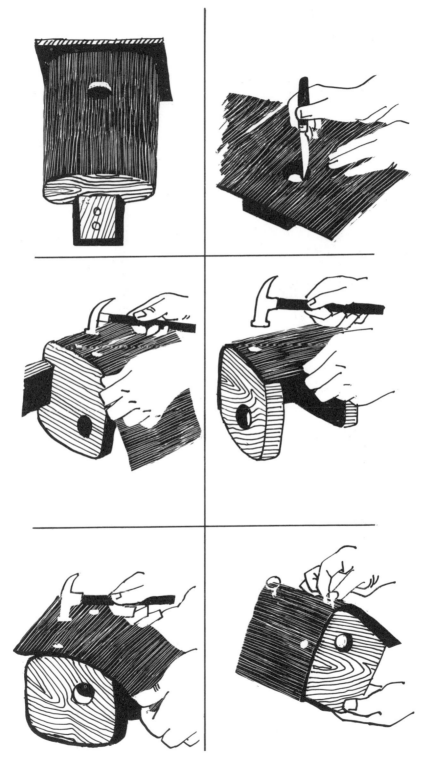

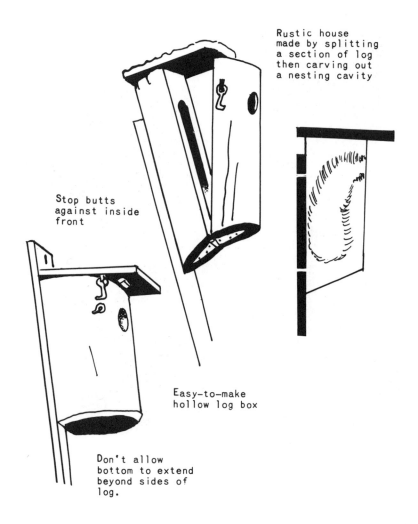

Rustic house
made by splitting
a section of log
then carving out
a nesting cavity

Stop butts
against inside
front

Easy-to-make
hollow log box

Don't allow
bottom to extend
beyond sides of
log.

the pot so the heads of the nails catch on the ridge and hold the pot tightly against the board.

Hang this pot on a fence post, clothespole, or tree trunk. House wrens have been attracted to this sort of house.

Florists sometimes sell large gourds, or perhaps you've

grown some in your own garden. The gourds must be dry to work right.

Carefully cut a hole of the right size for the bird you want in the gourd, which should be at least 6 inches in diameter. Hang the gourd in a tree with a piece of wire. Wrens, crested flycatchers, and swallows have used gourds for nesting boxes.

Building birdhouses and putting them out are fun in themselves. But it's nothing compared with the fun of watching the adult birds carry nesting materials into the house and later food to their young. Then comes the most fun of all — the day the young birds poke their heads out of the hole and finally flutter out to learn to fly.

If you build birdhouses this year and expect birds to use them again next year, be sure to clean them out. Remove all the old nesting materials and be sure the houses are dry and clean before you close them up again. You don't like an untidy or dirty house—neither do birds.

Eastern blue grosbeak. (Other name: blue pop.) *Guiraca caerulea caerulea.*

Woodpecker family. Picidae.

Nuthatch family. Sittidae.

Ruby-throated hummingbird. (Other names: common hummingbird, hummer, rubythroat, humbird.) *Archilochus colubris.*

Northern flicker. (Other names: yellow hammer, golden-winged woodpecker, yellow-shafted woodpecker, pigeon woodpecker, high-holer, wake-up, harry-wicket, wickup, clape, and possibly a hundred others.) *Colaptes auratus luteus.*

III Backyard Sanctuaries

In addition to birdhouses and feeders, there are two other methods of attracting birds to a backyard or park, both of which are as good as or better all year round than either birdhouses or feeders. The first is birdbaths and the second is plants of various kinds that attract birds.

Birdbaths

Many birds need water, as we do. They need it for drinking or for bathing. Birdbaths are easy to make or buy and are a very effective way of attracting birds to the yard. Birds will be attracted to water at all seasons of the year.

Probably the easiest way to make a birdbath is to start with a top of a garbage can or trash can. The top will act as the bath since it will hold water.

There are three ways of setting up the bath out in the yard. The easiest way is merely to lay it on the ground, pack some dirt around it to keep it steady, and fill it with water. But neighbors' dogs may drink the water, or cats may try to catch the birds that go there for a drink.

A better way is to get a 4-foot-long piece of 4-by-4-inch wood or 2-by-4-inch and drive it into the ground so it stands up perfectly straight. Remove the handle from the can top, and throw it away. Fasten the can top to the top of the post with three large screws. Before pushing or

Garbage can
cover

Brick fastened
to cover. Handle
hung inside pipe

Section of
sewer pipe

hammering the screws through the can, place a rubber or leather washer on the screw. When you screw the screw in tight, the washer will prevent the water from leaking out. Another way is to paint the inside of the can top with two or three coats of good white enamel. The enamel usually seals the holes.

Another good way to mount the can top is to use a piece of clay sewer pipe (available at plumbing supply shops or lumberyards) about 8 inches in diameter. Set one end of the pipe a few inches in the ground so that it will not tip over.

Then find a rock or brick that will slide down inside the pipe. Fasten a piece of wire around the brick, and fasten the other end of the wire to the handle of the can top. The distance between the brick and top should be about 12 inches.

Place the can top on the pipe so that the brick hangs down on the inside of the pipe. The brick will keep the can top from blowing or falling off when birds perch on it.

Paint the pole or pipe dark green or white so that it blends in with the garden background. Also, be sure to place the bath near some shrubs so that birds can fly to cover if a cat or hawk comes by. When birds are soaking wet, they have a difficult time flying quickly too far.

It's also a good idea to place a large stone or rock in the middle of the bath for birds to perch on before they jump in for a bath or to stand on while they drink.

Sometimes it takes birds awhile to find the birdbath, and you may begin to feel that they will never find it. Here's a way to help them find it:

Use an old coffee can or other tin can, and hang it 2 or 3 feet over the birdbath. Using a small nail, punch a hole in the can just above the bottom rim. Whittle a small wooden plug, and insert it in the hole from the inside.

Fill the can with water. Adjust the plug so that the water drips out very slowly, a few drops a minute, into the bath. That drip, both the sound and the ripples on the bath, will attract birds.

Winter Birdbaths

Birds need water in winter, too, but cold weather frequently freezes the bath so the birds cannot drink the water.

You can make a freezeproof bath easily by using two old coffee cans, an electrical extension cord and socket, and a 10- to 40-watt bulb, depending on how cold it is.

Cut a small hole in one can. Push one end of the cord through the hole, and fasten the socket to it. Place the bulb in the socket.

Fasten a plug on the other end of the wire. Place the can on the outside windowsill or on the back porch railing if you have a porch light. Connect the plug to an electrical

A winter birdbath.

outlet in the house or on the porch so that the bulb lights up.

Place a second can on top of the first, and fasten it with wide tape. Run the tape around both cans where they meet.

Put water in the top can. The heat from the bulb will keep the water from freezing except in very cold weather, and birds will have water to drink all day long.

Providing Natural Food and Cover

Although birdhouses and feeders will attract birds at certain times of the year and birdbaths will attract them at any time, probably nothing is more attractive than the right kinds of plants.

71

Birds are wild animals. By instinct they feed on wild fruit, seeds, and insects and nest in natural places, such as trees, shrubs, or open fields. They will eat food you put out and will nest in man-made houses, but they prefer natural food and nesting sites to man-made substitutes. The people who have been most successful in attracting birds to backyard sanctuaries have done so by planting the right kinds of shrubs for food and shrubs that provide cover and shelter.

It does not require too much space devoted to shrubs to attract some birds. But generally, it is necessary for the shrubs to be planted in masses — that is, covering a solid area from the ground up to 7 or 8 feet high or higher. Here a shrub and there a shrub is better than nothing. But it is not as good as planting several shrubs in relatively small areas or even a row of shrubs or trees that birds can use as a "roadway" across the yard.

In thinking of shrubs that are attractive to birds, think of them as being in two groups: those that provide hiding places and shelter from enemies, and those that provide food. Fortunately, many shrubs that are attractive to look at are also good for birds.

Food Shrubs

Dogwood may grow as a shrub or a small tree, depending on what kind it is. But any dogwood is one of the best

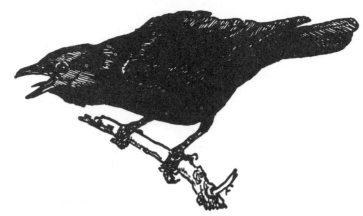

Crow (crow and jay family). Corvidae.

Starling family. Sturnidae.

Orchard oriole. (Other names: brown oriole, basket bird, swinger, orchard starling, orchard hangnest, bastard Baltimore.) *Icterus spurius.*

Baltimore oriole. (Other names: fire hangbird, firebird, oriole, golden robin, golden oriole, hangnest, Baltimore bird, peabird, hammock bird.) *Icterus galbula.*

food plants for birds you can find. It has attractive blossoms in the spring, and even in winter some kinds have reddish, greenish, or yellowish stems and twigs that are colorful. It will grow almost anywhere. More than ninety kinds of birds are known to eat the fruit (berries) on dogwood; they include quail, flickers, bluebirds, catbirds, thrashers, robins and other thrushes, waxings, grosbeaks, sparrows, and purple finches.

Elderberry is another shrub that is used for food by many different birds. It has a purplish black fruit that may be used for jams or jellies. Some birds will nest in elder thickets if the shrub is large enough to provide good cover. Among the birds that eat elderberries are quail, woodpeckers, kingbirds, phoebes, mockingbirds, catbirds, thrashers, bluebirds, vireos, grosbeaks, towhees, thrushes, and sparrows.

Wild rose will make an attractive hedge or fencerow in a yard. It grows as a low shrub or can be trained to grow on a trellis. When the blossoms are gone, you will see a red hip, as the seedpod is called, and this is what birds eat. More than forty kinds of birds feed on wild roses; they include grouse, quail, pheasants, thrushes, robins, and cardinals.

Blueberries, which may be low-growing shrubs or quite high shrubs, depending on location and kind, are easily grown in the yard or garden. They are well known as fruit and are prized by such birds as grouse, quail, bluebirds, chickadees, titmice, catbirds, thrashers, robins, thrushes, waxwings, orioles, grosbeaks, towhees, and king-birds.

Blackberries and raspberries are common fruit that we eat. They are easily grown in a garden or yard and are one of the best plants for birds. More than 150 kinds of birds are known to feed on these berries. They include thrushes, quail, sparrows, bluebirds, robins, grosbeaks, catbirds, woodpeckers, kingbirds, waxwings, vireos, orioles, cardinals, and towhees. The blossoms are known to attract hummingbirds.

Holly is an attractive shrub for any yard, since the leaves stay green all winter. At least forty kinds of birds will eat holly berries; among them are grouse, quail, sapsuckers, mockingbirds, bluebirds, thrushes, and waxwings.

These are only a few of many plants that may be used in backyards, gardens, or other areas to attract birds. The fruit of many of them stay on all winter and will provide food at a time when birds need it most.

Cover Shrubs

In the same way that most food shrubs can serve two purposes—beauty in the yard and perhaps food for you, as well as for birds—other shrubs provide nesting places for birds, as well as added beauty in the yard.

Generally small trees or shrubs that do not lose their

Pigeon (pigeon and dove family). Columbidae.

Wood duck. (Other names: wood widgeon, tree duck, summer duck, bride duck, bride, acorn duck.) *Aix sponsa.*

Eastern kingbird. (Other names: bee bird, bee martin, field martin, tyrant flycatcher.) *Tyrannus tyrannus.*

leaves in winter make excellent cover. That means trees or shrubs such as hemlock, cedar, or spruce.

Hemlock is used frequently as a hedge. It grows quite densely when the tops are cut back and makes an attractive hedge for a fence line. It provides good cover and nesting sites for several birds and even food for winter birds such as siskins or crossbills.

Cedar also makes a good fencerow or hedge and is easily grown. In addition to providing nesting sites for birds, it provides food for at least fifty kinds of birds—for example, robins, waxwings, thrushes, bluebirds, grosbeaks.

Spruces, when planted rather close together along a fence line or in clumps, are good for birds. Several backyard birds, including robins, jays, doves, and grackles, will nest in them. The seeds in the cones provide winter food for crossbills, siskins, and chickadees.

Yew is an attractive, generally low-growing evergreen shrub and, when it grows densely, will provide good nesting sites for birds. Its red berries also provide food.

One of the best shrubs for nesting sites in the yard is a rambler rose. It is especially good if it grows in a large clump or bush rather than on a trellis or arbor. Song sparrows seem to like roses for nesting sites, and since they often raise two broods of young a year, a dense clump of rambler roses will provide "music," as well as flowers, for most of the spring or summer.

How to Attract Hummingbirds

Hummingbirds will be attracted by many garden flowers or shrubs. Generally, however, they prefer blossoms that are reddish or orange in color.

Consequently, plants such as the azalea, columbine, phlox, delphinium, geranium, cardinal flower, scarlet runner bean, hollyhock, bee balm, and morning glory will attract these interesting tiny birds. It's well worthwhile to plant some of these easy-to-grow flowers just for hummingbirds — if for no other reason.

A variety of plants usually is better than a large number of plants all the same kind. If you have a yard or other place where you can set out some of these food and cover shrubs, you can easily have your own sanctuary — a place where birds will come to feed or nest every year. A natural sanctuary such as this is better than an artificial one and is much easier to care for.

But even if you cannot plant shrubs, knowing that birds use the plants for food or shelter can be helpful to you. Look around in neighbors' yards or in parks or public gardens for these shrubs or trees. Watch them regularly, and you will see more birds.

The Author

TED S. PETTIT is a well-known authority on natural history and conservation. He has long been associated with the professional staff as a member of the National Council of the Boy Scouts of America where he is currently director of conservation. He has a graduate degree in science education and biology, has worked on the editorial staff of *Audubon Magazine,* and has written many articles and books on nature hobbies and conservation. Mr. Pettit is an avid photographer, fisherman, camper, hiker, canoeist, and all-around outdoorsman. He and his family live in Somerville, New Jersey.

Index